TIMELINES OF
AMERICAN HISTORY ™

A Timeline of the Jamestown Colony

HISTORY
OF THE
UNITED STATES,
FROM THEIR
FIRST SETTLEMENT AS ENGLISH C
IN 1607, TO THE YEAR 1808,
OR
THE THIRTY-THIRD OF THEIR SOVEREIGN
INDEPENDENCE.

BY DAVID RAMSAY, M. D.

CONTINUED TO THE TREATY OF GHENT,
BY S. S. SMITH, D. D. AND L. L. D.
AND OTHER LITERARY GENTLEMEN.

IN THREE VOLUMES.

VOL. III.

PHILADELPHIA:
PUBLISHED BY M. CAREY,
FOR THE SOLE BENEFIT OF THE HEIRS OF THE AUTHOR.
1817.

Janell Broyles

rosen
central™

The Rosen Publishing Group, Inc., New York

To my teacher Mrs. Roberts, who made history matter to me

Published in 2004 by The Rosen Publishing Group, Inc.
29 East 21st Street, New York, NY 10010

Copyright © 2004 by The Rosen Publishing Group, Inc.

First Edition

Library of Congress Cataloging-in-Publication Data

Broyles, Janell.
A timeline of the Jamestown Colony/Janell Broyles.—1st ed.
        p. cm.—(Timelines of American history)
Summary: Provides a chronological look at the history and development of Jamestown Colony in Virginia.
Includes bibliographical references and index.
ISBN 0-8239-4536-7 (library binding)
1. Jamestown (Va.)—History—17th century—Juvenile literature. 2. Jamestown (Va.)—History—17th century—Chronology—Juvenile literature. 3. Virginia—History—Colonial period, ca. 1600–1775—Juvenile literature. 4. Virginia—History—Colonial period, ca. 1600–1775—Chronology—Juvenile literature. [1. Jamestown (Va.)—History—17th century. 2. Jamestown (Va.)—History—17th century—Chronology. 3. Virginia—History—Colonial period, ca. 1600–1775. 4. Virginia—History—Colonial period, ca. 1600–1775—Chronology.]
I. Title. II. Series.
F234.J3B76 2004
975.5'4251—dc22

2003013103

Manufactured in the United States of America

On the cover: Jamestown Fort, Virginia, circa 1608. This is one of the earliest settlements in America.
On the title page: Journal page, dated 1607-1608, from History of the United States, detailing life in the first settlement of English Colonies.

Contents

1

The New World

According to legend, a Norseman named Leif Eriksson was the first European to visit America. He sailed from Norway to Greenland and then to a place he named Vinland. More than 500 years later, an Italian explorer named Christopher Columbus wanted to find a sea route to India for Spain, and instead of traveling east over land,

Leif Eriksson was the son of famous Norseman Erik the Red. This painting shows Eriksson and some of his crew off the coast of the land he would call Vinland. His crew consisted of thirty-five men.

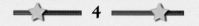

he sailed west across the Atlantic. He thought he could reach India this way. Instead, he landed in the Bahama Islands. Other explorers realized that he had found a whole new land—America.

1000
Leif Eriksson discovers Vinland. Though historians are not sure, they think Vinland extends from the East Coast of the present-day United States to the Hudson Bay in Canada. A colony of Norwegian settlers is founded, but the people die off.

October 1492
Christopher Columbus makes the first of four trips to the New World. He sails to the Bahamas, Cuba, and Haiti. Later, he explores Central America and the West Indies. He never admits that he didn't really find India.

Spanish explorer and navigator Amerigo Vespucci was born in Florence, Italy, in March 1451. Even as a young boy, he wanted to travel and see what the world looked like. Both North America and South America are named after him. He died in 1512.

1499
Amerigo Vespucci explores the coast of South America and discovers that it is a continent, not a part of India or Asia. Mapmakers in Europe draw maps of the new land and name it "America" after him.

5

Europe and the New World

Once countries such as Spain and France heard about the New World, they rushed to declare it for themselves. Sadly, they did not care about the rights of the people who already lived there. They killed hundreds of Native Americans in battles over land and gold. Also, the arrival of the Europeans exposed the Native Americans to diseases like smallpox, and many died. The Europeans set up settlements, planted crops, and built churches. Sometimes they lived peacefully with the Native Americans, but usually there was fighting.

★ **September 1513**
Vasco Nuñez de Balboa discovers the eastern shore of the Pacific Ocean and claims the land for Spain.

★ **1521**
Hernán Cortés overthrows the Aztec Empire with the aid of horses, steel weapons, and cannons.

★ **1524**
Giovanni Verrazano explores the coast of North America. He is the first European to see Manhattan Island.

★ **1531**
Francisco Pizarro conquers the Incas of Peru. Like Cortés with the Aztecs, Pizarro had better weapons

This map of both North and South America was created in 1590. It features images of famous explorers Christopher Columbus, Amerigo Vespucci, Ferdinand Magellan, and Francisco Pizarro.

than the Incas. Smallpox had weakened the Incas, and they could not fight very well.

1533 ★

Jacques Cartier sails into the Gulf of Saint Lawrence, leading the first European expedition up the Saint Lawrence River. He lands on the Gaspé Peninsula and claims the land around the Saint Lawrence River for France.

The First English Colony—Roanoke

Sir Walter Raleigh was an important man in England. He decided to send settlers to start a new colony on Roanoke Island. The first group Raleigh sent returned to England after a year. Nobody knows what happened to the second group of settlers. In 1590, their village was found empty by Captain John White. All that was there was the word "Croatoan"—the name of a nearby island—which was scratched on a tree. Captain White sailed to Croatoan, but no one was there.

★ **June 24, 1585**
Sir Walter Raleigh sends the first English colonists to Roanoke Island, near what is now North Carolina. This is the first English colony in North America. Because they do not know how to grow their own food, they try to make the local Native Americans feed them. There is not enough food for everyone, and fighting breaks out.

★ **June 18, 1586**
Sir Francis Drake stops at Roanoke on his way back to England. The colonists ask him to take them back with him, and he agrees.

★ **August 1587**
Sir Richard Grenville and 150 colonists arrive at Roanoke. Once again, the new settlers try to set up a colony.

8

A briefe and true report of the new found land of Virginia. of the commodities and of the nature and manners of the naturall inhabitants. Discouered by the English Colony there seated by Sir Richard Grenuile Knight In the yeere 1585. Which Remained Vnder the gouernement of twelue monethes, At the speciall charge and direction of the Honourable SIR WALTER RALEIGH Knight lord Warden of the stanneries Who therein hath beene fauoured and authorised by her MAIESTIE and her letters patents: This fore booke Is made in English By Thomas Hariot seruant to the abouenamed Sir WALTER, a member of the Colony, and there imployed in discouering.

CVM GRATIA ET PRIVILEGIO CÆS.MA.ᵗⁱˢ SPECIA.ᴸⁱ

FRANCOFORTI AD MOENVM TYPIS IOANNIS WECHELI, SVMTIBVS VERO THEODORI DE BRY ANNO CIƆ IƆ XC. VENALES REPERIVNTVR IN OFFICINA SIGISMVNDI FEIRABENDII

Thomas Hariot lived in the colony of Roanoke Island from 1585 to 1586. This is a page of text he wrote about life in the colony. The report was called *A Briefe and True Report of the New Found Land of Virginia*, and it described the land and the Native Americans Hariot saw.

1590 ★

Captain John White returns to Roanoke Island and finds the settlers gone.

2

Settling Jamestown

King James I of England was a very smart man who wrote many books. He is famous for creating the King James Bible, which was translated into English from the original Greek and Hebrew. James believed that the power of kings came from God. He thought that since he wanted the English to conquer America, then God wanted that, too.

James sent the colonists to Virginia to do three things: find gold, settle the land, and find a way across the New World to Asia. He thought that the Native Americans, who were there first, had no right to their land.

This is a portrait of King James 1 of England. He was born in 1566 to Mary, Queen of Scots, and Henry Stuart, Lord Darnely. James's mother was the queen of France before her first husband, Francis II, died. James died in 1625.

March 24, 1603

Queen Elizabeth dies. King James VI of Scotland, her cousin, becomes King James I of England.

This is a seal that was created for the Virginia Company. The seal was used like a signature is used now to sign important documents. The image on the left is of King James.

1604

King James publishes "A Counterblaste to Tobacco," which calls smoking a "filthy custome." Just a few years later, tobacco imported from America would make England very rich.

1606

King James designs a new flag for England by combining the flags of England and Scotland.

June 1606

King James charters the Virginia Company, whose job is to start colonies in the New World. It sets up a council and appoints a governor to run the new colony. It also finds settlers, supplies, and ships.

The Colony Is Founded

Being a colonist was not easy, but colonists were necessary if England wanted to be a powerful country. England needed people to build settlements in the new colony, farm the land, and send the crops back for sale. The Virginia Company looked for colonists to start new towns in America. It printed stories that said America was a wonderful place full of gold and treasure. Many poor people and criminals signed up to go to the new colony. They thought life in America would be easy and that they would become rich. But only a few of them survived.

This woodcut shows what Jamestown looked like when the settlers founded it. Life was very difficult for the early settlers. They had to learn new ways of doing everything, from finding food to learning how to build homes with what little was available in the new land.

★ **December 20, 1606**
One hundred four settlers set out in three ships from England to start a new colony on Jamestown Island, off the coast of Virginia.

This is what the Jamestown fort looked like after the settlers built it. It had high walls on all three sides to protect them from attacks from the Algonquin Native Americans who were already living there. They would steal guns and other supplies, and they would shoot bows and arrows at the settlers hoping that they could scare them off their land.

January 1607 ★

John Smith is put in chains by the other ships' captains, who think he wants to cause a mutiny. They unchain him when they get to Jamestown.

May 12, 1607 ★

The settlers land at Jamestown and start building a fort.

June 15, 1607 ★

The settlers finish building the fort. To make the walls, they stand tree trunks upright. The fort is triangular, with a watchtower at each point.

Problems in the New Colony

Most of the Jamestown colonists did not know much about farming or finding food. The food they brought with them soon ran out. Instead of learning how to grow food, they spent their time drinking, fighting each other, and searching for gold. They wanted the local Native American tribe, the Powhatans, to supply food for them.

At first, the Powhatans were afraid of the colonists' weapons and agreed to help them. But the more food they gave the colonists, the less the tribe had to eat. Soon, fighting began to break out every time the colonists wanted more food. These struggles lasted many years.

★ **September 10, 1607**
The Council, which runs Jamestown, accuses settler George Kendall of causing problems in the colony.

★ **September 12, 1607**
The Council finds its president, Edward M. Wingfield, guilty of lying about what Kendall did and takes away his title. John Ratcliffe takes his place.

Captain John Smith, who was one of the seven council members in charge of the new colony, became the president in 1608. He was born in 1580 in Willoughby, England.

December 10, 1607
John Smith and his men travel up the Chickahominy River in search of food. They are captured by the Powhatan tribe. Some of Smith's men are killed.

December 29, 1607
John Smith is brought to the chief of the Powhatans, who is called "the Powhatan." The Powhatan's daughter, Pocahontas—meaning "playful one"—saves Smith's life. Her real name is Matoaka. She already knows Smith; she had tutored him in the Powhatan language.

In 1607, Pocahontas, the Powhatan's daughter, saved Captain John Smith. He had been out exploring the region when he and some fellow settlers were captured. He was about to be killed with a club when Pocahontas saved him.

15

3

Hard Times and Tobacco

As it turned out, Jamestown Island was not the best place to build a town. Because there was not enough fresh water to drink, the colonists became sick. The land was swampy and filled with mosquitoes. Some mosquitoes carry a disease called malaria, and many colonists died. Some people in the colony

The Jamestown settlers had to work extra hard because the land was so swampy. This was even more difficult because of the original 105 passengers on the Jamestown voyage, twenty-nine were gentlemen and none were farmers. These were not men used to hard work.

worked hard, but others did nothing. This caused a lot of fights. Without everyone working, there would not be enough food to eat in the winter.

Some colonists believed they would soon find gold, go back to England, and be able to buy everything they wanted. They were wrong.

★ **January 1, 1608**
John Smith returns to James Fort and finds that only thirty-eight settlers are still alive.

★ **January 2, 1608**
Smith is accused of causing the deaths of his men, and the Council wants to hang him. Just then, new settlers arrive with a supply of food. Their captain, Christopher Newport, keeps Smith from being killed.

★ **February 1608**
Smith and Newport meet with the Powhatans again. They trade beads for food.

★ **Summer 1608**
Smith decides that someone needs to make sure that the crops are planted and harvested. He forces the settlers to work. This makes them so angry that they force him to leave.

17

The Starving Time

The winter of 1609–1610 in Jamestown was called the Starving Time because so many settlers died of hunger. The settlers had not grown enough corn to eat. The Powhatans were tired of giving away their food, and they refused to continue helping the settlers. The settlers were trapped. They tried to survive by eating rats, dogs, and anything else they could find, but most of them starved.

This image from 1609 shows a settler handing out a small amount of corn to a large family. Though there are women in this picture, there were very few women in the colony at this time. The first woman in Jamestown, Anne Frost, sailed over on a supply ship that came to the colony in 1608.

1609–1610

During the winter, more than 400 settlers starve to death. However, even before the winter, many of the colonists were weak from malaria and diseases they had brought with them from England. By the spring of 1610, only 60 remain. Most of them are very weak and sick.

May 23, 1610

The survivors of the ship *Sea Venture*, which was wrecked at Bermuda, finally arrive in Jamestown. They are shocked to find so few colonists.

This is a reproduction of the *Sea Venture*, one of six ships that set sail from London with supplies for Jamestown on June 2, 1609. The commander of the ships was Sir George Somers. The *Sea Venture* was wrecked close to Bermuda on July 28, 1609.

June 7, 1610

All the settlers leave Jamestown to go back to England.

June 8, 1610

Before they get very far, the settlers meet three ships from England filled with new settlers who are on their way to Jamestown. Since the new ships have supplies, everyone decides to return to Jamestown.

Tobacco Saves Jamestown

Nothing was going right for Jamestown. New groups of settlers kept arriving, but many died. The survivors could not find anything valuable to send back to England. One group of settlers found a lot of mica, a shiny rock with gold flecks. They thought it would be worth lots of money. They sent it to England, but it was worthless. Then John Rolfe discovered that tobacco grew well in the soil of Jamestown Island. The Virginia Company sold the tobacco for a profit. Jamestown finally started to pay off.

1611
John Rolfe imports the first tobacco seeds to Jamestown from Trinidad.

1612
John Rolfe teaches the colonists how to grow tobacco. They find that tobacco grows very well in the warm, humid air of Virginia. However, it is very hard work. Soon after, most of the settlers are growing tobacco and sending it to England.

1616
The Virginia Company begins to give 50 acres of land (20.2 hectares) to any settler who pays for his boat trip from England. Settlers get 50 more acres for any family members or servants they bring.

Once the colonists were producing lots of good tobacco crops, they began to export tobacco. This image shows barrels filled with tobacco being loaded onto a ship in 1615. The settlers sold their tobacco in England, where they made a lot of money.

1616 ★
The number of settlers in Virginia begins to rise.
In 1616, there are 350. By 1650, there would be 13,000.

July 30, 1619 ★
The General Assembly meets in
a Jamestown church to establish a new government
for Virginia. It creates laws for the settlers.

4

Jamestown from 1622 to Today

The Powhatans were not the only tribe near Jamestown. The Algonquin Native Americans were also fed up with the settlers taking their land and with their animals eating their crops. In 1622, they attacked Jamestown and killed more than 300 colonists.

When this news reached King James, he thought the Virginia Company was doing a poor job. He decided to make Jamestown a royal colony, which he would oversee. Then Jamestown did well for many

The 1622 attack of the Algonquin Native Americans on Jamestown became known as the Jamestown Massacre. As this image shows, many of the settlers were taken by surprise. However, because the colonists had guns, they killed most of the Algonquin.

years. However, it was still not the best land to farm or live on. When the statehouse burned down in 1698, the settlers decided to move to other villages. Jamestown was abandoned.

★ **March 22, 1622**
The Algonquin attack Jamestown and kill 357 colonists, but they are defeated. Later, their village will be wiped out by colonists.

★ **1624**
King James makes Jamestown a royal colony. He also appoints a governor to rule it.

★ **1676**
Nathaniel Bacon, a farmer, leads a rebellion against Governor Berkeley. Bacon doesn't think Sir William Berkeley is protecting the farmers from attacks by the Native Americans. Bacon burns down Jamestown and forces Berkeley to run away. After Bacon gets sick and dies, Jamestown is rebuilt.

★ **1698**
Jamestown's statehouse, where the General Assembly meets, burns down.

★ **1699**
Williamsburg becomes the capital of Virginia.

23

The American Revolution

Jamestown was the first permanent English colony in America. But it was just one of many colonies. New settlements were created along the eastern coast of America. The Native Americans were pushed farther west or died out as more Europeans came to the New World. Cities like Philadelphia and Plymouth grew in size and wealth. England still made all the laws for the colonies. But after many years, the colonists decided they wanted to make their own laws. England would not let them. War broke out, and when it was over, the colonies become the United States of America.

★ **1732**
Massachusetts, Rhode Island, Connecticut, New Hampshire, Maine, Maryland, North Carolina, South Carolina, Georgia, New Jersey, Pennsylvania, Delaware, and New York are all settled colonies by this time.

★ **September 5, 1774**
The First Continental Congress meets in Philadelphia to talk about unfair English taxes.

★ **April 19, 1775**
The American and British armies fight at Lexington and Concord, beginning the American Revolution.

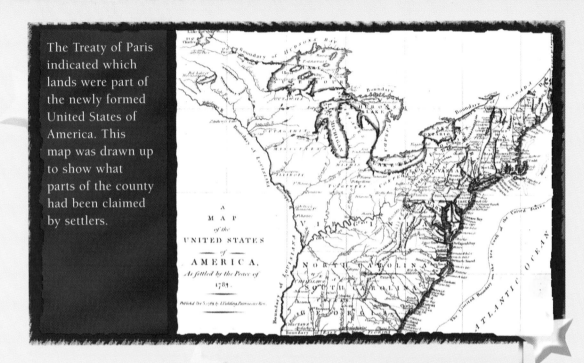

The Treaty of Paris indicated which lands were part of the newly formed United States of America. This map was drawn up to show what parts of the county had been claimed by settlers.

May 10, 1775 ★
The Second Continental Congress meets in Philadelphia. They begin writing the Declaration of Independence.

July 4, 1776 ★
The Declaration of Independence is adopted. It says that the colonies can create their own government. It is signed in August.

September 3, 1783 ★
The American Revolution ends when Britain and the United States sign the Treaty of Paris.

Jamestown After the American Revolution

For many years, the site where Jamestown used to be was nothing but farmland. Buildings fell down, and weeds grew. The forest grew again. All that could be seen of the old town was a brick church tower and the gravestones in the cemetery.

As of today, the wall of the first Jamestown fort as well as parts of other buildings have been uncovered. Jamestown is an important part of American history. Everything we learn about it helps us understand what life was like for those very first settlers.

The image on the left shows the remains of the Jamestown colony. The image on the right shows various tools that were used in the colonies, as well as old keys and locks. When archaeologists dug up the site, they studied the tools and objects they found to get a sense of how the colonists lived and survived.

1861
Confederate soldiers build a fort on Jamestown Island during the Civil War.

1893
Mr. and Mrs. Edward Barney give some land (that used to be Jamestown) to the Association for the Preservation of Virginia Antiquities.

1909
A statue of John Smith is set up in Jamestown. In 1922, a statue of Pocahontas is added.

This is an image of Pocahontas after she converted to Christianity and married Jamestown settler John Rolfe. After her marriage, she changed her name to Rebecca, but she would always be remembered as Pocahontas. She died in 1617.

1934
The rest of Jamestown Island becomes part of the Colonial National Historical Park.

1994 to present
Historians begin to explore Jamestown. They dig up the island, looking for pieces of Jamestown's history. They find many old items, such as belt buckles and spoons, left over from colonial times. They are still uncovering parts of old Jamestown today.

What Is a Timeline?

A timeline is a list of dates showing when important events happened. Events are listed by date from the earliest to the most recent. We make timelines so we can understand history and remember which events happened first. Timelines also help us understand how one event might have caused another one to happen. A timeline can have a lot of information or just a little. Historians make a lot of timelines to help them understand different periods in history. But anyone can draw a timeline—maybe you should try it!

Glossary

abandon (uh-BAN-dun) To leave without planning to come back.

antiquities (an-TIK-weh-tees) Things that are old, like coins or buildings.

claim (KLAYM) To say something belongs to you.

colonize (KAH-luh-nyz) To settle in a new land and claim it for the government of another country.

conquer (KON-ker) To take over.

continent (KON-tin-ent) One of the seven great masses of land on Earth.

Continental Congress (kon-tin-EN-tul KON-gres) A group of American colonists who got together to create the new American government.

council (KOWN-sul) A group called together to discuss or settle questions.

explorer (ek-SPLOR-ur) A person who travels and looks for new land.

General Assembly (JEH-nuh-rul uh-SEM-blee) A group of people who began meeting to make laws for the Virginia colonists in 1619.

A Timeline of the Jamestown Colony

governor (GUH-vuh-nur) A person who is in charge of a company or a region.

mutiny (MYOO-tin-ee) A rebellion against the people in charge, usually on a ship at sea.

profit (PRAH-fit) Money earned by selling something for more than it cost you to make it.

rebellion (ruh-BEL-yun) A fight against one's government.

smallpox (SMOL-poks) A serious and often fatal sickness that causes a rash and leaves marks on the skin.

tobacco (tuh-BA-koh) A plant whose leaves can be dried and smoked or chewed. Tobacco contains nicotine, which is very addictive.

Treaty of Paris (TREE-tee UV PAR-es) An agreement signed by the United States and Britain in Paris, France, on September 3, 1783. Britain agreed that the United States had the right to be its own country.

wealthy (WEL-thee) Having a lot of money.

Web Sites

Due to the changing nature of Internet links, the Rosen Publishing Group, Inc., has developed an online list of Web sites related to the subject of this book. This site is updated regularly. Please use this link to access the list:

http://www.rosenlinks.com/tah/jaco

Index

A Timeline of the Jamestown Colony

Credits

About the Author: Janell Broyles works in children's publishing in New York City.

Photo credits: Cover, pp. 5, 9, 11, 13, 15, 16, 19, 21, 22, 24, 26 © Hulton Archive/Getty Images; p. 1 © Special Collections Research Center, University of Chicago Library; pp. 4, 10, 12, 14 © Bettmann/Corbis; p. 7 © Corbis; p. 18 © Lawson Wood/Corbis; p. 27 © National Park Service, Virginia/Library of Congress.

Designer: Geri Fletcher; Editor: Annie Sommers